CREATIVE
COLOURING
for kids

Buster Books

T0015796

Illustrated by Cindy Wilde
and Emily Golden Twomey

First published in Great Britain in 2022 by Buster Books,
an imprint of Michael O'Mara Books Limited, 9 Lion Yard,
Tremadoc Road, London SW4 7NQ

W www.mombooks.com/buster   f Buster Books   🐦 @BusterBooks   📷 @buster_books

The material in this book previously appeared in *Amazing Copycat Colouring*,
Beautiful Copycat Colouring and *Brilliant Copycat Colouring*.

A CIP catalogue for this book is available from the British Library.

ISBN: 978-1-78055-833-2

2 4 6 8 10 9 7 5 3 1

This book was printed in May 2022 by
Shenzhen Wing King Tong Paper Products Co. Ltd.,
Shenzhen, Guangdong, China.

FSC
www.fsc.org

MIX
Paper from
responsible sources
FSC® C010256